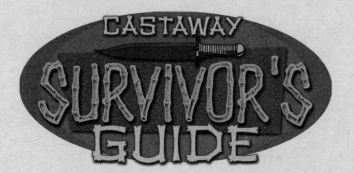

RORY STORM

SCHOLASTIC INC.

New York Toronto London Auckland Sydney
Mexico City New Delhi Hong Kong

For the Boys

Acknowledgments

Many thanks to Phil Pennefathers for his invaluable Pidgin translations and to Lucy Irvine for her much appreciated contributions to this book.

ISBN 0-439-27151-7

Text copyright © 2000 by Rory Storm.
Copyright © 2000 by The Chicken House.

All rights reserved. Published by Scholastic Inc., 555 Broadway, New York, NY 10012, by arrangement with The Chicken House.

12 11 10 9 8 7 6 5 4 3 2 1   1 2 3 4 5 6/0

Printed in the U.S.A.   40
First Scholastic printing, January 2001

CONTENTS

WARNING!

This guide is to learn about extreme survival situations. The techniques are not suitable for use at home and are only to be used in real emergencies.

Rory

HOW
RESOURCEFUL
ARE YOU?

HOW RESOURCEFUL ARE YOU?

The difference between living and dying, making a success or making a misery of being a castaway, lies principally in your state of mind and your ability to draw on your own reserves.

If you are positive and believe you can make the most of a situation, you will do well in any environment (not just in survival situations). But to be a good castaway, you must also be resourceful, innovative, and able to think laterally — that means approaching problems from different perspectives.

So let's see how well you fare with this simple questionnaire to establish whether or not you're cut out to be a Castaway Survivor.

Oh, and by the way, don't worry too much if you don't appear to be natural castaway material. There are plenty of tips and advice throughout the book so that by the final castaway quiz, you should be at the top of anyone's survivor list!

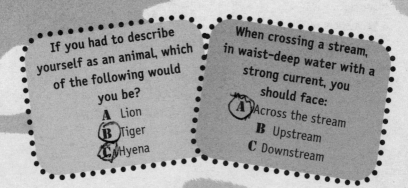

If you had to describe yourself as an animal, which of the following would you be?

A Lion
B Tiger
C Hyena

When crossing a stream, in waist-deep water with a strong current, you should face:

A Across the stream
B Upstream
C Downstream

An elderly lady gets onto a crowded bus and stands shakily in front of you. Do you:

A Stand up and offer her your seat?

B Give her your seat and go off in search of a spare seat farther down the bus?

C Ask her to move to one side so you can stretch your legs?

In your school, are you:

A Able to get along with most of your classmates?

B A bit of a loner, preferring to have just a few close friends?

C Class snitch? You have lots of acquaintances, but prefer to run with whoever is popular at the time.

You are in "snake country." Your best action to avoid snakes is to:

A Make a lot of noise with your feet.

B Walk softly and quietly.

C Travel at night.

If there is a new kid in the class who doesn't know anyone, do you:

A Introduce him/her to your circle of friends and try to include him/her in events and activities?

B Assume s/he'll approach you if s/he wants to be friends, but are friendly if s/he makes the first move?

C Give him or her a hard time just to amuse and please the class bullies?

Unarmed and unsuspecting, you surprise a large bear prowling around your camp. As the bear rears up about thirty feet from you, you should:

A Run.

B Freeze, but be ready to back away slowly.

C Climb the nearest tree.

You hear someone's cries for help and realize that a young girl is stuck in a muddy bog. Do you:

A Sacrifice your own clean clothes to lay branches over the mud, then wriggle across them on your stomach to pull her to safety?

B Make a mental note that this part of the woods gets muddy in wet weather and you should take a different route next time. Then go and call for help?

C Stand and laugh at the girl's

Your dad clears out the backyard shed and says you can use it now. Do you:

A Make it into a clubhouse for you and your friends?

B Use it as a place to get away and to have some privacy or solitude?

C Turn your nose up and wonder why anyone would want to spend time in a damp and drafty backyard shed?

If your mother gives you half a glass of cola, do you:

A Thank her and ask her if she'd like to share it?

B Decide the cup is half full rather than half empty and drink it gratefully because you're thirsty?

C Demand that she get you a full can of cola right now?

You decide to walk out in the wild country by following a series of ravines where a water supply is available. Night is coming on. The best place to make a camp is:

A Next to the water supply in the ravine.

B Midway up the slope.

C High on the ridge.

5

SCORING

Let's see how you fared with our castaway questionnaire. First, add up how many A answers you gave, how many Bs, and how many Cs. Then compare the totals.

If you scored mostly A answers:

You are a team player — considerate, a natural mediator, and thoughtful. You are a good person to have in any group activity. You tend to be sociable and well liked and are comfortable with most people. As a good communicator, you are able to make yourself understood and to help others understand one another's point of view.

You don't mind taking the lead but can also follow and support someone else's leadership. You have pretty good judgment about survival skills. You are an ideal candidate for being a castaway in a small community, although you probably also have the resourcefulness to do well in an individual situation. Well done! You show signs of good castaway promise.

If you scored mostly C answers:

Well, well, well. What have we here? Let me tell you that if you turned up in my unit with your attitude, you'd be out on your ear. At best, you need to polish up your people skills. At worst, you sound like a thoroughly selfish person. Shape up or ship out, matey, because no one would want you in their castaway community, but you may well find your classmates chipping in with their hard-earned allowance just to get you sent off to a deserted island!

If you scored mostly B answers:

You are a bit of a loner and an original thinker. You are self-reliant, like to do things for yourself, and are reluctant to rely on others. You challenge authority not simply for the sake of it but because you believe your ideas are just as valid as theirs are. Although you don't shun company, you are happy to be on your own. When in a group situation, you prefer to be in charge rather than working under someone else's leadership.

Almost certainly, you would do very well if you were shipwrecked and washed up as a lone castaway on an island. Your knowledge of survival skills is not bad at all. If you found yourself in a castaway community, you would have to make an effort to communicate well with the others, but I'd say you've probably got what it takes to be a castaway.

If you scored roughly equal numbers of A and B answers:

You're a good all-arounder. In fact, just the sort of person who'd do well as a castaway, whether you were in a community or on your own. You are a lateral thinker, inventive, content with your own company but just as happy to mix with others. You keep a cool head in dangerous situations and are an asset to yourself and the team. You also have good survival skills under your belt.

So how did you score? The category you fell into doesn't matter too much at this stage. By the end of this book, you'll probably discover a side to your personality that you never even knew existed. So let's get down to the nitty-gritty and learn some castaway skills, shall we?

In case you're wondering, the answers to the survival questions in the quiz are as follows:

3a. If you walk quietly or at night, you're likely to surprise an unsuspecting snake, and, in defense, it may bite you.

6b. A bear can move surprisingly fast and can outrun you and probably catch you before you get to a tree. Staying calm and backing away slowly is your best hope of avoiding attack.

9a. You present less resistance to the current if it hits you side on. So head straight across and be determined.

12b. You could get flooded out next to the water supply; at the top of the ridge, you'd be very exposed and would be battered by the winds. Pick halfway for good measure.

SO YOU WANNA WANNA BE A CASTAWAY?

SO YOU WANNA BE A CASTAWAY?

As a young boy, I was a huge fan of Robinson Crusoe, and I dreamed of being left to fend for myself on a deserted island. Thanks to my training with the Special Forces, that dream became a reality, and throughout my career, I've spent many months surviving off the land, either alone or with a couple of "comrades" while on dangerous missions.

I found out through experience that being a castaway isn't always the paradise that we automatically imagine. For a start, it can be extremely lonely being the only person on an island, not to mention a bit scary and possibly very dangerous. Alternatively, if you are cast up on deserted shores with a group of strangers, you might find that they drive you absolutely crazy and you'd actually prefer to be alone.

Even so, I bet if you took a vote among your classmates, the vast majority would still say Yes! to the chance of becoming a castaway on a heavenly island. And can you blame them? Who could resist the temptation of all that adventure? Not me, that's for sure! Glorious sunshine, deserted tropical beaches, palm trees, and best of all, no school.

But on a more serious note, finding enough food, water, and shelter, and avoiding being eaten is quite a challenge for anyone. So that's why we're going to look at some of the essential survival skills that will make your chances of being a successful castaway a whole lot better.

WHAT TO EXPECT

In this book, we'll look at ways for you to provide yourself with the lifesaving fundamentals of shelter, warmth, and food. And once you've got a few of these skills under your belt, you should be able to set up camp and survive just about anywhere.

As a castaway, you may only have one crack at being picked up, so you better make sure you are seen. That's why you'll also learn all about communications and signaling, as used by emergency services and the military all over the world.

IT HAPPENED TO ME

Once you've boned up on the basics of castaway survival, you'll have a chance to see how a few brave souls have had to put this theory into practice. The stories of real-life castaways will inspire you, and they may also give you some helpful hints when it comes to answering the "what if . . ." scenarios throughout the book.

As if there hasn't been enough excitement already, you'll also get the chance to "do it for yourself" with the castaway brainteasers, where you can wrack your brains to see if you can come up with the best survival plan to save you and your companions. And just to make sure that you haven't been sleeping on the job, there's a test at the end to check your survival and castaway knowledge.

INNER STRENGTH

Whether you choose to be a castaway and take yourself off to a remote isle or whether you find yourself marooned due to misadventure, you will need more than just survival skills. You will have to draw on your personal strength of will and character to make the most of your castaway status. After all, you may be in this situation for quite some time.

Ask any outdoor specialist and he or she will tell you that courage, inner strength, resourcefulness, initiative, and innovation are just as important as knowing some basic survival skills when it comes to living in the wilderness.

In fact, there's one more category I'd like to add to the list, and that's a sense of humor. The famous 1980s castaway Gerald Kingsland (who, sadly, died earlier this year) once found himself steering a leaking dinghy with a plank off an island full of crocodiles. When he dropped the plank, he exclaimed, "This is the story of my life! Up the creek without a paddle." This ability to see the funny side of life got him and many other survivors through their ordeals and the harsher moments of life. It will help you out, too.

CHAPTER TWO

GETTING STARTED

Whether you find yourself alone à la Robinson Crusoe or in a team, being a castaway doesn't have to be half bad, given the right climate, environment, and mental approach.

As you'll see from the following stories, the key to being a successful castaway is a belief in yourself and your ability to survive, a positive mental approach, tenacity, innovation, and some luck — not forgetting a few basic survival skills that will come in very handy. So let's get down to business, shall we?

BASIC CASTAWAY SKILLS

SHELTER AND WARMTH

BASIC CASTAWAY SKILLS

Regardless of the temperature or terrain in which you find yourself, when you first become marooned, your immediate need is for shelter and warmth. "But what if it's a sun-soaked tropical or desert island?" I hear you cry.

Well, you still need shelter from torrential rainfall, not to mention the blazing midday sun. And don't forget that even a hot climate can get very cold at night, so you will need some protection.

A fire is essential not only for warmth and to cook food but also to deter any unwelcome visits from local wildlife. After all, until you've done a complete "recce" (that's slang for "reconnaissance," a survey or observation) of your island home, you don't know what dangerous beasts and creepy-crawlies are out there! A controlled fire should keep them at bay . . . at least, let's hope so.

TEMPORARY SHELTER

Unlike in a survival scenario, as a castaway you have to make the assumption that you could be in this situation for a considerable time. You therefore want to make your base camp as comfortable and safe as you can. This requires planning and due consideration. In the meantime, you will need a temporary shelter.

A ROOF OVER YOUR HEAD

It is important to know how to construct a basic shelter in the outdoors. Here's a quick set of directions on how to construct a makeshift tent.

Using a sheet of plastic or canvas (perhaps a sail salvaged from a wrecked boat), a waterproof poncho, or a groundsheet, plus some cord, rope, or twine, you can make a comfortable shelter.

1 Find two sticks that are roughly the same length, preferably with a fork at one end.

2 Push them into the ground.

3 Tie your cord to the top of one stick, using the fork to keep it from slipping down. Pulling it taut, stretch the line across to the other stick, and tie it there.

4 Throw the sheeting over the line, and weight down the edges with heavy rocks.

This simple shelter has saved my bacon on several occasions, but don't worry too much if these materials are not easy to get. You can find temporary shelter in all sorts of places if you look around and use your imagination.

A cave is the obvious choice, but make sure it's not already occupied by tenants such as snakes, wildcats, or bears before you take over as principal occupant. If the cave is near the shoreline, be especially careful. You don't want the water to rise into the cave with the tide, effectively cutting off your escape route.

An upturned boat or life raft will keep you protected from the worst of the elements. When you don't have anything suitable to make a shelter, rely on natural cover such as trees, bushes, hollows, and rocks to provide some protection against the wind and rain.

Castaway Know-how

Before erecting your shelter, clear the ground of stones and twigs, and flatten the area by stamping down any lumps so you'll have a better night's sleep.

CHOOSING A CAMPSITE

During your first few days as a castaway, if food and water are in good supply, you can turn your attention to finding the ideal place to set up your camp. Do a good reconnaissance of your island home, and watch what happens to certain locations when the weather changes or at different times of the day.

CHAPTER THREE

Your camp is going to be a permanent base, so you don't want to rush into choosing the spot. Here are some pointers that you should take into consideration when choosing a location for a camp:

- You need to be close to a supply of fresh, clean water.
- There should be a plentiful supply of wood nearby.
- You don't want to choose a spot that is frequented by wild animals, so avoid game trails.
- Avoid setting up camp in a basin where cold air tends to settle or floodwater may flow.
- Try to find fairly level ground because it's not very comfortable living and sleeping on a slope.
- If you set up camp on the shore, make sure the high tide cannot reach you.
- Don't build your camp under trees where branches could break in high winds and crash down on you.
- Avoid solitary trees, which attract lightning.
- If you are camping near mountains, don't build your shelter in the path of a possible avalanche or rockfall.

CHAPTER THREE

You can make your permanent camp out of any durable materials you can find. Use driftwood, branches, and rocks. If you have some canvas, make it as secure as possible by binding it with rope, rags, or strips of leather. Alternatively, you can weight a structure using large stones.

Castaway Know-how
Build your shelter with the entrance facing away from the wind.

USEFUL TOOLS

You may need tools to help you build your shelter. If you don't have any manufactured tools (rescued from the ship), you can make your own stone tools by hitting one stone against another. Drop a flint against a rock and it will break, giving you a sharp cutting edge. Bones, antlers, and horns also make effective digging implements or hammers.

A good pocketknife is a useful piece of equipment to carry with you in the wild and could make life as a castaway much easier. But in the absence of such a precision-made cutting tool, you can make your own saw from a few items you might find while out beachcombing:

You'll need:
- A short piece of wire
- Some wood or string

1 Bend a loop in each end of your piece of wire.
2 Attach loops of string to the ends of the wire or wrap the ends of the wire securely around two small pieces of hardwood (toggles).
3 Using the looped pieces of string or toggles as handles, pull the wire

backward and forward in a sawing action.
4 Keep the wire taut, pulling straight, never at angles. Also, don't stand under the branch — you might get hit on the head when it falls!

Castaway Know-how

Ribs from a small animal are ideal for making into a crude needle to make your own clothes. Use dried animal intestines or fish gut as thread.

CAMP CRAFT

It makes no difference whether you're on your own or in a small group, to be a successful castaway, it's important to run an organized camp. Even a lone survivor needs to set a routine and some regular objectives, whether they're practical or just for fun.

If you're in a castaway group, then work out a roster so that everyone gets his or her fair share of dirty jobs and easier tasks.

Castaway Know-how

If you're marooned as a group, always leave at least one person in the camp to operate your signaling system in case a search plane appears. When foraging for food, hunting, or reconnoitering, always use the buddy system, working in pairs or more if numbers permit.

GOOD CAMP PRACTICE

You want your camp to be a safe and hygienic retreat where you can relax and unwind after a hard day of surviving off the land. If this is to be the case, there are a few safety precautions and disciplines that every good castaway should get in the habit of observing.

SAFETY

➤ Make sure sparks from your fire cannot reach any flammable materials in your shelter.

➤ Never leave the fire unattended.

➤ Don't prepare or cook meat or fish in camp. Gut and skin animals or fish near your traps to attract game to snares rather than to your camp.

➤ Store food well away from your tent in case wild animals come scavenging.

CHAPTER THREE

➤ Decide on a collection point for drinking water, and make sure no one washes upstream from it.

➤ Animals will also be attracted to any food waste, so always clean and pack everything away as soon as you've finished using it.

➤ Make your camp toilet downwind from your shelter. Believe me, you'll be grateful.

➤ Never site your latrine (camp toilet) near your water supply.

➤ Make a latrine cover to keep out flies, and always replace it, even if you're a lone castaway.

➤ Indelicate though it may be to mention, wild animals are drawn to the smell of human waste. So make sure you cover feces with earth after you've done the business.

➤ When a latrine starts to smell, dig a new one. And don't forget to fill in the old latrine.

Fact File
Soldiers don't use soap, wash their hair, or use antiperspirants or after-shave for at least three days before going into the jungle because it is the scent of these toiletries that attracts mosquitoes.

CHAPTER THREE

HOME COMFORTS

"Any fool can be uncomfortable" is a saying that you may have heard, and in essence it means that only an idiot suffers unnecessarily. With that in mind, the first thing you'll want to make for your castaway camp is a bed. After all, there's nothing like an uncomfortable night to guarantee you'll be grumpy and disspirited in the morning — and keeping up morale is essential.

MAKING AN A-FRAME TUBE BED

1 Drive two pairs of sturdy sticks into the ground at an angle, leaving a distance of slightly more than your height between the pairs.

2 Lash or tie the top of each pair together to create an X shape (also called an A-frame).

3 Make a tube of strong material (the material from a sail is perfect), sewn or pinned together. You can even use a heavy-duty plastic sack that you've opened at the bottom.

4 Choose two strong, straight poles slightly longer than the distance between the two A-frames, and pass them through the tube of fabric.

5 Place the sticks over the frames so they rest on the sides with the tube, preventing them from slipping any lower.

6 Hey, presto! A bed fit for a king or queen.

Alternative

If material is in short supply, securely lash the two long poles to the A-frames and lay branches across the two poles. Then cover this platform with softer bedding such as branches, moss, hay, or leaves. Remember to change the bedding regularly.

Personal Hygiene: Although keeping clean is probably the last thing on your mind when you become a castaway, in fact it's pretty important. I've been on exercises with the guys when we haven't been able to wash or change our clothes for weeks. Take it from me, after a day or so, your friends don't smell so good, and after a few more days, you begin to smell yourself — and it ain't pleasant.

If you get unkempt and smelly, it's bad for morale. So take a few minutes out of your day to get clean.

Wash your clothes in fresh water away from your drinking supply, and tie them to a tree in a windy spot to dry if you can't rig up a clothesline.

Castaway Know-how

If the ground is too hard or rocky to drive the A-frame supports into it, you can make the bed secure by lashing cross-members between the feet of each A-frame and between the two A-frames.

MAKING A FIRE

So you've sorted out the first order of business for surviving in the wild, which is shelter from the elements. Now you have to turn your attention to the second vital element, which is warmth.

If you can light a fire anywhere under any conditions, then you'll always have a source of warmth and protection, a means of cooking, and last but not least, a way of signaling to rescuers.

A WIGWAM FIRE

1 Clear an area of leaves, twigs, dry grass, etc.,
until you've got bare ground.
2 Make a small pile of kindling (twigs, small
sticks, and small, dry leaves).
3 Around this, build a wigwam shape with
thin but longer sticks.
4 Put a ball of tinder (dry grass, dead leaves, or bark)
inside the kindling. Light the tinder with a match.
The kindling will soon catch.
5 Once your fire is lit, it will burn fiercely. The
wigwam will collapse into a pile of hot, burning
embers. Now, very carefully, add more sticks.

Castaway Know-how

Once your fire is burning well, add thin sticks for
cooking. Thick sticks are best for slow-burning fires to
sit around and keep warm.

Castaway Know-how

When it's wet, you can find dry deadwood in
the cracks and branches of trees or underneath
bushes and piles of leaves.

LIGHTING A FIRE

Matches are far and away the easiest way to
light a fire, but a box won't last you long, so
castaways have to find other ways to make a
spark to start a fire. If fuel is in plentiful supply,
many castaways keep a fire burning at all times
to avoid the need to repeatedly start a fire.

There are many different ways to start a fire
without matches. If you become a castaway,

the following methods of lighting a fire will be useful.

1 Hand Drill

➤ Cut a V-shaped notch in any hardwood, preferably a flat piece so you can lay it down like a baseboard and keep both hands free.

➤ Put a little tinder in the V notch.

➤ Make a slight depression or small hole at the top of the V.

➤ Use the stick made of softwood (one with a soft, pithy core) for a spindle, and place it in the hole.

➤ Roll the spindle back and forth between the palms of your hands, running your hands down it as you press it into the depression.

➤ When the friction makes the spindle tip glow red, blow gently to light the tinder.

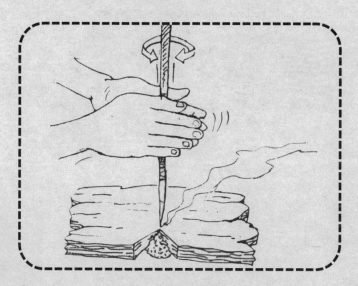

CHAPTER THREE

2 Sunlight Through a Lens

➤ Use a magnifying glass, eyeglasses, or a camera lens.

➤ Focus the sun's rays to form a tiny, bright spot of light. Keep it steady and shield it from the wind.

➤ Blow gently until it glows.

3 Flint

➤ Strike the flint with anything made of steel, and sparks should fly.

➤ Blow gently when the sparks touch the ball of tinder.

Castaway Know-how

If you're on a pebbly beach, light your fire above the tide line. Wet or porous rocks can explode when heated, causing nasty injuries. Avoid rocks that have been under the water or that sound hollow when banged together.

Castaway Know-how

Dry animal droppings in the sun, and then mix with dried grass and leaves for an effective fuel for your fire. And don't worry — it doesn't smell too bad!

CASTAWAY
SKILLS

FOOD
AND WATER

CASTAWAY SKILLS

The third part of the survival triangle, together with shelter and warmth, is nourishment. Although you can go for relatively long periods without food, you'll find that you will get weak without nourishment, and even the smallest task will seem like a huge challenge when you're extremely hungry. Nonetheless, you can get by for some weeks without eating, but you can only survive for a matter of days without water. So one of the top priorities of a castaway is to find a source of water.

FINDING WATER

Even if your food runs out, you can keep going for a very long time on water alone. So here's how you find a good source of water.

- Look in valley bottoms for streams. You can even dig in dry streambeds — the water may be just below the surface.
- At the coast, look for plants growing in faults on cliffs. You may find a spring.
- Plants often trap water in cavities. Don't forget to strain it to remove insects before drinking, though — you don't want dead flies slipping down your throat, do you?
- Tie clean cloths around your legs and ankles and walk through wet vegetation (particularly in the morning when plants are

covered in dew). These can then be sucked or wrung out.

➤ Melt snow a little at a time in a pot and gradually add more. (If you put a lot in the pot, a hollow will form at the bottom and you'll burn your pot.)

OTHER SIGNS OF WATER

➤ Virtually all mammals need water to survive, so if you come across an animal trail that looks well-worn and shows signs of use, following it can lead to water.

➤ Seed-eating birds make their way to a water supply in the late afternoon, so follow flocks of birds to see where they go.

➤ Ants, too, are always near water, so if you see a column of ants entering or leaving a hollow in a tree trunk or fallen log, there is a good chance that you'll find water inside.

COLLECTING WATER

Rainwater is the purest water you can drink when you're marooned, so try to collect as much as possible when it rains. Use your imagination to find containers, and fill them all. An upturned turtle shell is a good castaway container. Also look for plastic bottles washed up as flotsam, an empty tin can, or even bark from a tree. Use your imagination and improvise!

You can also collect dew in the morning using a large piece of sheeting such as a raincoat or even a nylon sail to catch the water droplets. Scrape out a shallow depression in the soil, line it with the material, and see what you get in the morning. If you're desperate, dew collects on metal and can sometimes be collected this way.

Castaway Know-how

Trees draw water from deep below the ground — deeper than you can dig. So why not let the tree do the work for you? If you have a plastic bag, tie it around a healthy, leafy branch. Evaporation from the leaves will produce condensation in the bag and water will collect in the bottom corner for you.

CHAPTER FOUR

FOOD, GLORIOUS FOOD

At last, you say, we come to food. Well, once you have taken care of your other priorities, you can turn your attention to nourishment, not so much because it's a necessity but because it provides comfort, warmth, and a sense of well-being. And you'll need it if you're marooned for any length of time.

Better still, thinking about food and planning how you're going to trap or forage for it can be a great way to take your mind off the fact that you're lost — and the results can be very satisfying.

Personally, I like nothing better than a meal that I've caught and cooked for myself over an open fire under the starlight — beats take-out fast food any day.

PLANTS AND FRUIT

It's important to know about these extreme survival techniques — BUT NEVER, IN EVERYDAY LIFE, EXPERIMENT WITH FOOD OR VEGETATION THAT YOU FIND IN THE YARD OR COUNTRYSIDE. The consequences are just not worth the risk.

However, as a castaway, you are not foraging for plants for fun but for survival, and so a few guidelines will be helpful.

PLANTS TO AVOID

- Don't eat fungi unless you're an expert. Some fungi can kill within hours.
- Don't eat anything that looks like beans or peas. They can be toxic.
- Don't eat bulbs unless they look, smell, and taste like onions or garlic.
- Avoid brightly colored plants — they're often toxic.
- Avoid plants with hairy leaves or stems, spines, thorns, or very shiny leaves — these contain irritants or are toxic.
- Avoid mature bracken, which can be lethal. Eat only the tightly coiled fronds called fiddleheads.
- Don't eat any plant that irritates your skin when you touch it, with the exception of nettles. Nettles that have been well cooked are very nourishing.
- Don't eat any plant with a milky sap (with the exception of dandelions).
- Don't eat any plant with umbrella-shaped blossoms.
- Don't eat any plant with white, yellow, or red berries.
- Don't eat any fruit that is in five sections.

CHAPTER FOUR

➤ **Don't eat anything in the wild that resembles a cucumber, melon, parsnip, dill, parsley, or tomato.**

Castaway Know-how
Many edible plants, such as dock leaves or dandelions, are bitter to the taste, so boil and then change water and cook for a short while longer to get rid of the bitterness.

SAFE FORAGING

You cannot assume that just because an animal has eaten a plant or fruit, it's safe. Sometimes animals can tolerate foods that will make us seriously ill. So always use the following edibility test on a plant or fruit before making it part of your castaway diet.

EDIBILITY TEST

This is the professional Special Services edibility test. **In everyday life, never eat**

1 LOOK: Check to be sure that the plant isn't slimy, worm-eaten, or too old and withered.

2 SMELL: Crush a small portion. If it smells of bitter almonds or peaches, don't touch it.

3 FEEL: Rub very lightly on the tender skin under your upper arm. If you experience any discomfort, a rash or swelling, then throw it away.

vegetation that you find in the yard or in the countryside.

4 TASTE:

So far, so good. Now, try the next routine, leaving 15 seconds reaction time between each step to see if you develop a reaction:

- Place a small portion on the lips.
- Place a small portion in the corner of your mouth.
- Place a small portion on tip of tongue.
- Place a small portion under tongue.
- Chew a small portion.

If at any time you experience any discomfort, throw it away.

SAMPLE:

Swallow a very small amount and wait five hours. Don't eat or drink anything else during this time. If no reactions are experienced, you can consider the plant safe to eat.

Castaway Know-how

If you get an upset stomach from something you've eaten, drink plenty of hot water and don't eat again until the pain has gone. If the pain is severe, try to make yourself vomit by pushing your fingers down the back of your throat.

A MOVABLE FEAST

The motto of the armed forces is "If it moves, eat it." That means that anything that swims, flies, walks, crawls, or wriggles is fair game, and this in turn means everything from insects and worms to rats and seagulls is on the menu.

INSECTS AND GRUBS

Before you turn your nose up, insects are found in virtually every habitat, and they are tasty, nutritious, and plentiful. So once you've overcome your initial squeamishness, you may well find that they become part of your castaway staple diet.

There are only a few rules to observe:

➤ **Eat only fresh insects.**
➤ **Avoid pupae you find in the soil.**
➤ **Avoid hairy caterpillars — they sting.**
➤ **Apply the plant edibility test.**

Insects and grubs taste best when cooked first — roasting them on thin sticks is the easiest. (They're ready to eat when they're dry, but of course you've got to catch 'em first.)

CHAPTER FOUR

BUG HUNTING

➤ A fire at night will attract various night-flying insects. (Remember to remove the wings before you eat them.) So at night, hang some thin material in front of a light or fire, and place a container of water underneath it. The insects are attracted to the light, flutter up against the material, and drop into the water. Their wings fall off, and all you've got to do is strain the bodies out and roast them over the fire.

➤ Hunt insects early in the morning when they are cold and sluggish, and you'll have a breakfast fit for a king or queen.

You'll find all manner of juicy bugs in the branches and hollow trunks of trees or under rocks and logs. Try to think Pumbaa and Timon from *The Lion King* here.

➤ Top of your delicacy wish list should be termites (remove wings first), termite eggs, beetle grubs or larvae, smooth caterpillars, grasshoppers, locusts, and crickets, but remember to take off the hind legs of these last three before eating because otherwise they scratch when you swallow them.

ANIMALS FOR FOOD

The beauty of insects is that even if you're injured, you should be fast enough to outrun a grub. However, catching prey that can outmaneuver and outrun you is not so easy. For this, you'll have to use your superior intellect.

You can eat the flesh of all mammals, birds, or reptiles (with the exception of toads), and their eggs make a tasty meal, too.

Some people don't like the idea of eating animals, so you need to make your own mind up about hunting and trapping wildlife.

Don't forget — only castaways hunt for food; in everyday life all animals should be respected and not hunted or harmed unnecessarily.

Fact File
Locusts and grasshoppers
contain almost three
times as much protein as
prime steak.

CHAPTER FOUR

TRACKING ANIMALS

Given practice, you can recognize the tracks of wild animals as easily as you can spot a horseshoe tread in the mud.

The easiest place to study animal tracks is in sand or snow because the prints are clear and easy to follow. Watch out, in particular, for the tracks of rabbits, which are distinctive because of the combination of long hind and short front feet. A good way to get experience at identifying tracks is to watch an animal when it is moving on sand, snow, or muddy ground and then to study the footprints it leaves behind. Start with the family dog or cat, and work up to squirrels, birds, and other wild animals.

CHAPTER FOUR

Another telltale sign for the experienced tracker is an animal's droppings.

I imagine just about all of us might recognize rabbit or sheep droppings, but did you know that you can even identify a bird by its droppings? Small and mostly liquid droppings indicate a seed-eating bird with water nearby, while small bits of bone or fur in its pellets suggest a bird of prey.

CHAPTER FOUR

FINDING GAME

- Look for trails between watering holes/feeding places and homes.
- Most mammals eat at night, so look for tracks in the early morning.
- Droppings provide a good clue as to the size and type of animal and what it eats. The bigger the pile . . . need I spell it out?
- Gnawed bark, discarded food, and the remains of prey reveal an animal's presence.

GONE FISHIN'

If you're marooned on an island, one of the most plentiful supplies of food comes from the sea in the form of fish and shellfish.

➤ In hot weather, fish retreat into deep, shaded water, and when it's cold, they seek shallow spots where the sun warms the water. Armed with this information you can choose the best time and place to try to catch a meal.

➤ You can improvise a hook from all kinds of materials — from bone and wood to bent pins and safety pins to thorns and nails. Fishing line can be made by unraveling a sheet of dry canvas and braiding the threads.

➤ Even without a hook and line, you can still improvise fishing equipment. By the sea, try building a semicircular wall from rocks or stones just below the high-tide line. As the tide goes out, fish are trapped behind the barrier.

A long, sharpened stick can also be used for spearing fish — standing above and swiftly stabbing down is the best method. Or why not improvise a net by attaching your shirt to the end of a forked stick and tying the top to form a bag?

Alternatively, cut the top off a large plastic bottle just below the neck. Invert the neck inside the bottle. Put bait at the bottom of the bottle to entice fish in. Once in, they can't get back out.

CHAPTER FOUR

Castaway Know-how

Make sure all fish are fresh and cook immediately. If the fish's eyes look milky, your fingers leave indentations in the flesh, or if it has no scales, discard it.

Fact File

Some saltwater fish are highly poisonous. Avoid any fish that is conical, that can inflate itself, that has a snoutlike mouth, that has spines, or that looks like a stone. Don't even touch them, let alone try to eat them!

COOKING FOOD

After all your hard work, you finally have something to eat, but unlike getting a hamburger from the freezer, it's not quite that simple in a castaway situation.

Before you can start cooking, you have to pluck, skin, or scale your prey, and take out its internal organs (gutting). This should always be done away from your camp or the scent may attract unwanted visitors in the night.

But it's not all bad news. Like all the best restaurants, you have several ways of cooking your food, which breaks up the monotony a bit.

CHAPTER FOUR

If you have containers, you can boil most of the foods you find or catch. You can roast small mammals or birds by skewering the carcass on a spit and turning it over hot embers. Alternatively, most food can be cooked by wrapping it in large, nonpoisonous leaves, grass, mud, or clay and roasting it in hot coals. Incidentally, when you remove the clay, any scales or skin will be peeled away with it, which saves you a job!

Cooking Snake

Cut off its head and at least another 3 in. (8 cm) of the body to remove all poison glands. Skin it by slitting along its underside and peeling off the skin. Remove the gut, and then wash the flesh and either stew it or wrap it in grass or damp leaves and cook it in mud.

SENDING
SIGNALS

SENDING SIGNALS

If you're shipwrecked, the chances are that you'll drift on the current before you're washed up on a remote shore. If this is the case, then you may be far from the shipping routes, which means that waving a white hanky at a ship more than a mile away is a complete waste of your time and effort — you'll never be seen like that.

So at this point, you should keep your hanky for blowing your nose and instead give some serious thought to how you could signal a distant ship or plane to make sure you're rescued.

SIGNAL FIRES

During the day, smoke is a great locator for rescuers. A plume of smoke rising into the skies can be seen by a rescue plane or passing ship from many miles away.

TO MAKE A SIGNAL FIRE

You learned how to make a fire in Chapter Three. The only way in which a signal fire differs from your cooking fire is the fuel you use. The basic procedure for lighting the fire is the same — you need tinder and kindling. However, once the fire is lit, you need fuels that create a lot of smoke.

Scout around to see what you can find. The obvious choice is green wood, but oil or rubber from such things as tires taken from a downed aircraft or the remains of a dinghy will do. Even shale from the beach, which contains a lot of oil, can be used to make smoke.

Set up three signal fires on high ground if possible, but not so far away from your camp that the rescue plane or ship will be gone by the time you get there.

Avoid building fires among trees where the canopy prevents the signal from being seen. Find a clearing if you're in a wooded area.

Check the direction from which the wind normally blows, and build your fire downwind of any other signals you've laid out to be seen from the air. If you're lucky enough to have space for a helicopter landing site, clear it of obstacles and make sure that the smoke from your signal fire is downwind of this, too, so that a helicopter pilot can see where he or she is landing.

FLASHBACK

Another great way to signal over long distances is by using light. You may well have salvaged a flashlight, which is useful at night. Remember to ration the use of your precious batteries, only signaling when there's a good chance of the signal being seen. Most of the time, you should use your fire instead.

During the day, you can rely on anything reflective such as glass, a mirror, or a piece of shiny metal to flash a rescue signal.

Any sort of distress signal will do — but once you're sure you've made contact with someone, you may want to send an urgent message. To communicate a message by signaling, you should try Morse code, which is universally recognized.

MORSE CODE

Here's the alphabet in international Morse code. Remember, a long flash is a dash, and a quick one is a dot.

A	.-	N	-.	1	.----
B	-...	O	---	2	..---
C	-.-.	P	.--.	3	...--
D	-..	Q	--.-	4	....-
E	.	R	.-.	5	.....
F	..-.	S	...	6	-....
G	--.	T	-	7	--...
H	....	U	..-	8	---..
I	..	V	...-	9	----.
J	.---	W	.--	0	-----
K	-.-	X	-..-		
L	.-..	Y	-.--		
M	--	Z	--..		

Probably the most important word to memorize is .../---/... — which is SOS — and everybody knows that SOS means "send help."

Fact File
Almost any signal repeated three times is understood internationally as a distress signal.

CHAPTER FIVE

RADIO PROCEDURE

If you're living in an elective castaway community, then you'll probably have access to a radio transmitter or satellite phone. These should be used sparingly but can be lifesavers in emergency situations.

Would you know what to do if you had to send a message for help? Well, most sets come equipped with instructions on how to use them, but there are certain procedures that you should follow to make sure your message gets through loud and clear.

- Prepare your message before you transmit it so that you don't get flustered, repeat yourself, or forget to say something vital. Write it out if necessary, or just jot down the points you need to make.
- Remember to say who you are calling and to tell the person who you are before you start your message (e.g., "Hello, Solomon

Islands, this is Pigeon, over." Or "Hello, all stations, this is Pigeon, over.")

🐚 When you've finished what you're saying and you want to wait for a reply, say "over."

🐚 When you've finished your message/ conversation completely, say "out."

🐚 Key words that are understood by radio hams everywhere are: "Mayday" = "help, I'm in distress"; "Roger" = "understood"; "Okay" = "okay" (this may seem obvious, but "yes" is not universally understood, whereas "okay" is).

If you need to spell words to make sure you're understood, you should use the alphabet that is used internationally by the military and emergency services — you'll undoubtedly have heard it used on cop shows and hospital dramas on the TV.

A = alpha; B = bravo; C = charlie;
D = delta; E = echo; F = foxtrot; G = golf;
H = hotel; I = india; J = juliet; K = kilo;
L = lima; M = mike; N = november;
O = oscar; P = papa; Q = quebec;
R = romeo; S = sierra; T = tango;
U = uniform; V = victor; W = whisky;
X = x-ray; Y = yankee; Z = zulu.

If you were spelling "Pigeon," it would read "papa, indigo, golf, echo, oscar, november."

You'll soon get the hang of it, and with a little practice you'll be able to spell using this alphabet as quick as a flash.

In fact, there's a good game you can play to practice the alphabet while riding in the car to school or wherever. Read out car license plates using the emergency services alphabet — that's how I perfected my skill (well, that and going on missions).

SORRY, WHAT DID YOU SAY?

You'll often hear a lot of crackling, static background sound (known as "squelch") when you're receiving a radio transmission. Most radio operators soon learn to tune out this background noise, but for the inexperienced, it's very distracting.

One way to practice tuning in to a vital message and screening out the rest is to get a friend to go into the next room. You then put on a radio or television for distraction and try to "broadcast" a message to him or her over the background noise. Then get back together and see just how much of your message he or she understood.

Castaway Know-how

Keep sending Mayday messages even if there is no reply or a lot of squelch. There's a chance your message is being received even though you can't hear a reply.

Fact File
Dinghies, life rafts, and even life jackets are often equipped with short-range transmitters, which considerably increase your chances of being picked up.

Message in a Bottle
Even the fabled castaway method of communication, the message in a bottle, is now known to work. This year, Jodene Prater, one of eight children taking part in the Castaway 2000 project (see Chapter Eight), wrote a note saying that she really missed chewing gum, popped it in a bottle, and flung it into the sea.

Mary McLeod, who lived on the neighboring island six miles away, found the message and bought chewing gum and candy and sent them to the grateful castaway. Now that's what I call successful communication!

CASTAWAY STORIES

CASTAWAY STORIES

Well, that's gotten some of the theory out of the way. Now let's whet our appetite for adventure with some real-life castaway stories. See whether you think you could manage as well as these brave souls in the same circumstances.

TAKING A RISK

In 1981, twenty-five-year-old Lucy Irvine answered an advertisement in an English newspaper. It read, "Writer seeks companion for a year on tropical island." It was the start of an amazing adventure.

She and the stranger met, and a few months later they were voluntarily marooned on the island of Tuin, off the northernmost coast of Australia, between May 1981 and June 1982.

During their year on the island, Lucy and Gerald were beset with dangers and difficulties. They survived despite a severe shortage of food and fresh water, shark attacks, dangerous wildlife, and debilitating illness.

UNABLE TO WALK

As usual, it wasn't the most obvious dangers such as crocodiles or poisonous wildlife that caused the biggest problems for the marooned pair. It was a series of tiny bites and cuts on their legs from sand flies and toxic coral that threatened to bring an early end to the adventure.

CHAPTER SIX

Unfortunately, the small open wounds got badly infected, and Gerald's lower legs began to swell so much that he could not walk for days at a time during their stay, leaving Lucy to do the foraging and fishing alone. Without the benefit of modern antibiotic medicines, the poison could not be banished, and the situation became very serious indeed.

Nonetheless, something worse was to come. Lucy explains, "Foolishly, I picked some attractive-looking beans when we were close to starvation and ate them before checking what they were. They were poisonous, and I became very ill.

"Because I was sick and had diarrhea at the same time, Gerald dug a trench at either end of me until the worst was over. Then he kindly helped me into the sea to wash. We were both pathetically weak but laughing at the same time. Later he said he was afraid I might die and he'd have to eat me, but there wasn't much worth eating because I was so skinny by then!"

DEADLY SPIDERS

If Lucy and Gerald had known more about the wildlife on Tuin, they might have been more scared. They shared a shelter happily with more than forty poisonous spiders, discovering that if they didn't disturb the spiders, the spiders didn't disturb them. Sharks were a nuisance when the castaways fished — they ate their catches — or when they swam, but they learned how to avoid them and killed them for food when they were hungry enough.

A LAWLESS TERRITORY

"It was certainly scary to know that if either one of us 'disappeared' — or even got murdered — nobody would know how it happened. But luckily we got on well as co-survivors most of the time," explains Lucy.

Despite all the difficulties, Lucy loved her castaway lifestyle. She says, "Life on Tuin was harder work than most people dreaming about life on a desert island imagine, but I still loved it. I'm glad I never thought it would be particularly easy, or I would have had a shock. Basic survival is time-consuming and tough — and if you take a break because you're tired, you might end up with nothing for supper. There's no Social Security or sick pay on a remote island — it's all up to you.

"Leaving Tuin at the end of the year and readjusting to 'normal' life was the hardest thing I've had to do. The truth is, I don't think I ever have 'adjusted' — that's why I was so keen to take my children off to another island some years later."

Do you think you'd be game enough to put yourself through another castaway adventure, or would it be a once-in-a-lifetime experience for you? It takes courage to face such a challenge twice, doesn't it? You can read more about Lucy's second adventure in Chapter Seven.

CHAPTER SIX

WHAT IF . . .

Do you know how you'd react if a poisonous snake or spider bit your only companion on the island? You wouldn't have long to think because every second counts once poison starts to spread through the body. Only your quick reactions could save your companion's life!

Despite what you may see in the movies, you should never try to suck the venom from a wound. Instead, try to get the victim to relax to stop the poison spreading. Apply pressure at the wound site, and immobilize the affected part.

Put a bandage above the bite and another bandage over that one (so if the bite is on the hand, start from the elbow and work down). Place the wound in cool water such as a stream, and try to not move the victim. Check the pulse and breathing, and be prepared to give artificial respiration if necessary.

Fact File
Fishermen in Samoa, in the South Pacific, developed a clever method of catching sharks. Making use of the shark's excellent hearing, they made a shark attractor of coconut shells halved and strung together on a stick. It was submerged under the water and shaken vigorously to lure curious sharks, which could then be speared.

CHAPTER SIX

LONG BEARD, PEDRO DE SERRANO

In 1540, a Spaniard called Pedro de Serrano was sailing in the Pacific when, for unknown reasons, his ship sank. He was plunged into the sea wearing only a shirt and a belt and armed only with a knife. He was the sole survivor.

He managed to swim to an island and dragged himself onto the shore. But Serrano's misfortunes were not over. The island had no vegetation, no shade, and no wood to build fires and shelter. Worse still, there was no fresh water — only sand that reflected the blazing sun and quickly absorbed any rain that fell during the brief but ferocious storms.

After a depressing first night, Serrano awoke determined to stay alive. He scoured the beach along the shoreline and found cockles and shrimps, which he ate raw.

DRINKING BLOOD

His biggest problem was his thirst, but he had a unique, if somewhat macabre, solution. He had spotted turtles not far from the shore, so he waited until they came within his reach and then seized them and turned them over on their backs. With no drinkable water and death hanging over him, he cut their throats one at a time and drank their blood.

Once he had slaked his thirst, he took the flesh from the shells and left it in strips in the sun to cure. He then cleaned the shells and let them dry. He used the shells to collect and store rainwater

— the biggest ones held something like eleven or twelve gallons!

MAKING A FIRE

Having solved the problems of food and water, Serrano set about the near-impossible task of building a fire. He had nothing to make a spark, so he went all over the island looking for a flint. Despite his careful search, he found none that were suitable. In his bleak new home there was only dead sand. Would you have given up at this point, or would you have had the determination to find a different solution, as Serrano did?

Undefeated, Serrano decided to search the seabed, diving until he found a couple of stones fit for his purposes. He pulled threads from his shirt and worked them into tinder. Collecting seaweed, seashells, and odd bits of driftwood, he managed to make a fire. When the heavy rains came, he used the larger turtle shells to protect his precious fire. How resourceful is that!

After some time, Serrano's clothes fell apart, and his hair and beard grew so long that they reached to his waist. Most surprising of all, the hair on his body also grew so that he was "covered all over with bristles."

TWO'S COMPANY

After three years, a vessel was wrecked near Serrano's island, and another lone survivor was cast up on the shores of his island. Imagine his surprise when the new castaway saw Serrano — a naked creature, covered in hair with an immense mane and beard, skin burned red and peeling and encrusted with sand, salt, bits of shell, and turtle meat. The new castaway must have been terrified. Both ran away from each other, but eventually the two men came together and embraced.

The men were forced to exist side by side in a small place, facing the harshest of difficulties. They took turns standing watch, looking for a rescue ship. After a while, they fought, and each moved to different parts of the island. But soon they put aside their differences and pooled their resources again.

RESCUE AT LAST

During their four years together, they saw many ships, but none saw their signal fires. At last, a vessel came close enough to spot their signals. The captain sent a small craft toward the shore, but when the sailors saw the two castaways (the second man had also become naked and grown very hairy), they were terrified — and began rowing back to their ship! Serrano and his companion cried out for them to come back and kept chanting Jesus' name over and over so the sailors would know they were Christian men. Fortunately, the seamen turned back and picked up the two castaways.

CHAPTER SIX

And so they were saved and taken aboard the boat, to the amazement of the crew. Pedro de Serrano and his fellow castaway sailed for Spain, but unfortunately the second castaway died on the voyage. Serrano lived, however, and made a considerable amount of money by showing his long hair and beard and recounting his amazing story in the courts of Europe.

He never lived to enjoy his wealth, though. He sailed back toward South America to collect a settlement in Peru, but before he set foot on land, Pedro de Serrano died of unknown causes.

If ever a man deserved to enjoy the good life after all he'd been through, it was Serrano. But, sadly, it wasn't meant to be.

Fact File

Many early castaways were sailors who had been put ashore and left by their ships because of some crime they had committed. This was the most serious punishment a man could be given. Whippings were routine and "walking the plank" was considered a quick and kind end compared to being marooned.

As you can see, life at sea in the 16th, 17th, and 18th centuries was extremely tough. Sailors would be away at sea for years at a time and in the harshest of conditions. For example:

Moldy biscuits and pickled pork and beef were the main food served. Maggots and weevils often had to be picked out of the biscuits before they were eaten.

Ships were full of lice, cockroaches, and rats.

Officers usually slept in bunks, but sailors had to bed down on the deck.

Crews had to bring along their own clothes, and they rarely got a chance to wash them.

Men drank beer and cider since few of them trusted fresh water.

Illnesses such as scurvy, caused by poor diet, were commonplace.

SOUTH AMERICAN HOME

In 1704, Alexander Selkirk was the sailing master on a ship named the *Cinque Ports*. He and his captain were both irritable characters, and they argued fiercely. Once, in a fit of temper, Selkirk asked to be put ashore. Unfortunately for him, the nearest land was an uninhabited island called Mas a Tierra, where he had plenty of time to regret his impetuous request.

However, in one respect, Selkirk was fortunate. The island on which he was marooned was a virtual paradise. It was more than twelve miles long and almost four miles wide at its broadest point, and it enjoyed a good climate.

There were no venomous creatures on the island, only turtles and sea lions, as well as goats, rats, and cats, which came ashore from the pirates' boats that occasionally stopped there for fresh provisions.

DAYS SPENT HUNTING

At first, Selkirk hunted goats with the pistol he'd been allowed to bring off the ship. Before long, his ammunition ran out. He was forced to hunt using his only other weapon — a knife.

In the beginning, he went hungry, but with lots of practice and perseverance he became fast enough to catch even the fleetest goat. His nutritious diet — comprised of fresh meat, fruits, and vegetables — made him exceptionally healthy. He developed extraordinary agility and almost superhuman speed!

WELL EQUIPPED

Since he had been a voluntary castaway on the island, Selkirk was better equipped than most castaways were because he had the contents of his sea chest. His possessions included his bedding, his gun and knife, a hatchet, a kettle, a flint and steel (for making a spark), a flip jar, a Bible, some books on navigation, and his mathematical instruments.

Equipped with these, he made himself two huts

from pimento logs covered with long grass. He lined the walls of one with goat fur (a bit stinky, but it kept the hut warm in the cold winter) to serve as his study and sleeping quarters, while the other was used as a smokehouse and kitchen.

SOLITARY LIFE

Despite his relative comfort, like any other castaway, Selkirk still faced a solitary life. He filled his time largely by catching goats for food, reading his Bible, and exploring his island.

On his walks, he would carve his name on trees so that if he died on the island, his identity might be known. He also notched tree trunks to mark the passing of his days on the island. (Sounds familiar? Yes, Daniel Defoe based *Robinson Crusoe* partly on Selkirk's story.)

LIFE-THREATENING ACCIDENT

Once, while hunting a goat, Selkirk and his quarry fell over the edge of a cliff. Fortunately, Selkirk fell on top of the goat, which cushioned his fall. The goat died, and Selkirk was knocked unconscious for at least a day. Eventually, he came to his senses and crawled painfully the mile or so back to his hut where he lay for ten days.

After this experience, he was terrified of falling ill or becoming injured because he knew that if he couldn't hunt or gather food he would die.

CHAPTER SIX

NEAR RESCUE

At this time, England was at war with Spain, so when some Spaniards landed on the island unexpectedly, Selkirk hid himself rather than be rescued. He reasoned that he preferred a lonely death to the fate of being a Spanish captive. He was sure they would kill him outright or work him to death as a prisoner.

So he kept his watch, and four years and four months after he had so rashly asked to be put ashore, an English ship came by and picked him up. By chance, one of his former shipmates from the *Cinque Ports* was on board and he recommended him to the captain who, in turn, offered him a position as mate.

Castaway Know-how
In 1768, Captain Cook's ship, the
Endeavor, charted the Pacific,
using navigational tools such as a
compass and a chronometer.

To make your own compass, stroke
the tip of a sewing needle along one
end of a magnet several times.
Tie a thread around the middle of the
needle so it hangs horizontally and can
swing freely. When it stops swinging,
the tip will be pointing north.

WHAT IF YOU WERE A CASTAWAY?

WHAT IF YOU WERE A CASTAWAY?

Some of those real-life castaway stories are pretty scary, huh? Yet despite the odds being against them, each of those marooned men and women survived while scores of other castaways have perished.

Why do you think that might be? Is it because they had luck on their side? Well, luck plays its part, I suppose. Did they have superior survival skills compared to the others? Undoubtedly, this can help to save your life, but in most of the stories we've just heard, the castaways were not experienced outdoor specialists at all.

Of course, knowing some basic survival skills will help you in a castaway situation (and that's why we're going to discuss a few more tricks of the trade in this chapter), but the real secret to their survival was their attitude of mind.

Despite the harshest of conditions, none of the castaways mentioned in Chapter Six were prepared to give up or be defeated by misfortune. They were all tenacious, resourceful, and prepared to improvise to make the best of their circumstances. And that is exactly what you must do if you are to be a successful castaway.

And don't forget, a sense of humor is really important, too! Whenever possible, you should try to have some fun, like our next castaways.

PIGEON POST

Nearly seventeen years after leaving Tuin, Lucy Irvine returned to a remote island in the South Pacific, but this time she was accompanied by her two sons, Benji, age eight, and Joe, age ten. Her eldest son, Magnus, age thirteen, had won a scholarship to boarding school, and he joined the family on his vacations.

The five-acre island, called Pigeon, is situated in the Outer Solomon Islands, more than a thousand miles off the coast of Queensland, Australia. Apart from the local islanders, an eighty-year-old Englishwoman named Diana Hepworth still lives there, having decided in the 1940s to raise her family on the island, away from the modern world. One of her sons is married to an islander, and they and their children also live in the scattering of islands that makes up Temotu Province.

ROUGH CROSSINGS

The Irvine family's adventure got off to a bad start when the small open boat taking them on the sea-crossing to their new island home nearly capsized in rough seas. They feared for their lives, and Benji, in particular, wondered what he'd let himself in for. But the freedom of the island proved irresistible to the boys, and Lucy soon relaxed back into the liberty and self-determination of being on a remote island.

The boys' education could not be put on hold for a year, so it was arranged that they would study for a few hours a day in a class of seven, with local children, and the lessons would be conducted in the tiny island school, which was made of leaves. Also, in their year on the island, they learned a whole lot more about life than any school could teach.

OVERCOMING PROBLEMS

That's not to say that the venture was without its dangers and low points. There were terrifying moments when the islands were battered by devastating torrential storms — and once there was a cyclone.

One of the hardest moments came when Benji suffered a serious wound from a machete while cutting open a coconut. He needed stitches and had to be taken miles in a dugout canoe for the wound to be treated. There are no western doctors in these island communities, although knowledge of local medicinal plants and herbs is still used to good effect among the islanders. Once, Lucy drank a preparation of tree bark to bring down a fever, and both boys were given drinks made from leaves to protect them from harm and make them strong.

FUN AND FRIENDSHIPS

Each of the Irvine boys forged great friendships with local kids. They would go off fishing with their newfound friends and stay for sleepovers with the island families.

They became so fluent in pidgin that they had no problems communicating with the islanders.

The boys became accomplished swimmers and divers, and each of them was able to explore the islands on their own in the kayaks that Lucy had brought for them — which they often swapped for locally made dugouts.

There were sharks and ferocious moray eels in the waters around the islands, so danger was ever present, but they learned when and where it was safe to swim. At night they speared parrot fish at the side of a coral cliff under the sea, and if a reef shark came along, a grown-up islander with them would chase it away — or kill it for its fin.

A DIFFERENT AGE

Time took on a whole new meaning on the island. Watches were useless, and waking up at dawn to go swimming was not unusual.

Life was very different for the Irvine family in the Outer Solomons. Their concerns had totally changed from when they were back home. They had new priorities and new views on what life and love meant. The year passed all too quickly, but the memories and the lessons they learned from their stay on Pigeon will remain with them forever.

Would you have liked to trade places with the Irvine boys? (You'll have a chance to try your hand at pidgin in Chapter Eight.) Could you swap watching TV and playing on your Play Station for spearing fish and collecting coconuts? These are considerations that you'd need to think about before committing to such a venture. For my part, there's no contest — the freedom to do my own thing and be my own boss far outweighs the luxuries of "civilized" society.

TREATING A MAJOR WOUND

What if you cut yourself very badly with a machete or knife like Benji did, and there was no outside medical help? Would you know what to do so you didn't bleed to death? These few essential actions could save your life:

- If you or a fellow castaway cut yourself badly and bleed profusely, wipe the wound thoroughly. Apply pressure to the wound, and bind it up with a bandage or cloth.

- If the dressing isn't soaked immediately with blood, leave it for twenty-four hours — then gently tease off the dressing and expose the wound to the air, which is nature's healing agent.

- However, if it keeps bleeding, repeat the process of applying pressure and a bandage.

- Still blood everywhere? Pinch the wound together, and tie around it in many places along the wound. Do NOT try to stitch it.

- Once the bleeding has stopped, inspect the wound, and clean it if necessary. Dead tissue and any pieces of fat should be cut away and foreign bodies picked out carefully. (Live tissue bleeds gently, dead tissue doesn't.)

TIP: Don't be squeamish about cleaning the wound — it's only the edges that hurt. Believe it or not, you can cut away the inside tissues without any pain.

Fact File
Wounds need to heal from the inside out, so even deep wounds should be left open. One of the major causes of gangrene among the Argentine forces in the Falklands conflict of 1982 was the immediate stitching of deep wounds by inexperienced medics.

CASTAWAYS IN AN ICY WASTELAND

Elmo Wortman and his four children lived a secluded life near the town of Craig, in north Alaska. This small community was far removed from any city comforts, and they lived off the land in a remote, harsh environment.

A trip to the dentist meant sailing 180 miles over some of the roughest water in North America, to Prince Rupert in British Columbia, then driving 96 miles inland to the dentist's office.

DISASTER STRIKES

On February 13, 1979, Elmo was returning home with his family, Jena, age twelve, Randy, fifteen, and Cindy, sixteen, after a trip to the dentist. (Margery, the eldest child, was staying with friends.) Elmo Wortman, who had the flu, was in his bunk, and Jena was at the wheel of the boat when the storm struck.

For thirty hours their yacht withstood the battering eighty-mile-per-hour winds and massive seas, but near midnight on February 14, the yacht foundered. The dinghy, which they had packed with survival provisions, was washed away, and they had to abandon ship.

Although Wortman was knocked unconscious, miraculously, they all survived.

A HASTY SHELTER

Washed up on the shore of a deserted coastline, they now needed shelter from the harsh winds.

They made a crude shelter and started a fire — amazingly, Randy still had some dry matches.

They went beachcombing and managed to find a few apples and some mussels, and by a stroke of luck the empty dinghy was also washed ashore.

Elmo worked out their approximate location and estimated that a cabin he knew of was no more than twenty-five miles away. From there, they could hitch a boat ride and get home safely.

That night they rested in their makeshift shelter, but the wind and snow made for an uncomfortable night's rest. The next morning, they patched together the damaged dinghy, which could carry only two people, and Randy and Jena started to paddle along the coast. Elmo and Cindy clambered along the cliff tops and made their way on foot. The going was very tough and cold, and they had to follow the shore around each deep inlet. Finally, they reached Randy and Jena, camped in a small cove.

RAFT-BUILDING

Dozens of logs lay strewn along the beach, so they decided to make a raft. Amazingly, it floated and they paddled off. The raft was soon caught in the full force of the wind and waves, and with everyone soaked with freezing water, they had to turn back and wait for better weather.

That night, they set off again, taking turns rowing. At dawn, the wind finally forced them ashore where they were stranded for another day. Once again, they boarded the raft but were beaten landward by strong currents. The little inlet where they landed was covered in more than two feet of snow and was extremely exposed.

Looking along the shore, Elmo could see what he believed to be Rose Inlet, where the cabin was located, only two or three miles away. Immediately, he decided that he and Randy should leave the girls on the shore and paddle the dinghy to the cabin to raise the alarm.

LEAVING THE GIRLS BEHIND

As he said good-bye, Elmo was aware that the girls had no food and no means of making a fire in this bleak wilderness. He promised they would be back in three hours. He left his daughters huddled under a sail on the beach.

As it turned out, Elmo was mistaken — it wasn't Rose Inlet they'd seen — but still he and Randy pressed on. The three hours in which they promised to return were long since gone. Eventually the mouth to Rose Inlet came into view, but night was falling and Randy was exhausted. They could see the cabin about fifty feet above the high-water mark, but the inlet was covered in sea ice, which forced them to walk the last mile.

They used the last vestiges of their energy to cross the ice — Elmo even fell in at one point — and when they finally reached the cabin, they collapsed with exhaustion.

To add to their despair, the radio was broken, but in the morning Elmo repaired it and transmitted a Mayday message. There was no response. Both men were experiencing excruciating pain as their frostbitten flesh started to thaw out.

ICY WAIT

Meanwhile, the girls were still huddled under the sail on the exposed beach. They had eaten bits of seaweed and sucked snow for water. They began to sing and recite the Lord's Prayer to give themselves some comfort.

Elmo and Randy felt sure that the girls must, by now, be dead. Not that they could move to rescue the girls anyway because of their swollen limbs and the extreme weather conditions.

At last, on the twelfth day after they had split up, the weather changed. Overnight, the snow and ice melted, the wind changed direction, and it started to rain.

Elmo and Randy launched a leaky motorboat hull they'd found. With one bailing while the other rowed, they set out to collect the girls' bodies. Leaving a note for the cabin owners, they took two sleeping bags and enough food for four days.

It was now three and a half weeks since the shipwreck and nearly fifteen days since the girls had been left on their own. Suddenly, the girls awoke to hear, "My babies, I've come back to get my babies," and lifted the sail to see their father.

SALVATION

Elmo could not believe that they were still alive. Randy heard the commotion and went hobbling up the beach to see his sisters and join in the remarkable reunion. The girls had to be carried to the boat, where they were wrapped in the sleeping bags. The family reached the cabin after dark. In the meantime, the owner had returned and, on reading Elmo's note, had left fresh groceries for them while he went for help.

The next morning, the Wortmans heard the sound of a helicopter, and their ordeal was over. Elmo Wortman lost half his right foot and all the toes on his left, and Cindy lost some toes. The girls said that they believed unwaveringly that their father would come back for them, and that's what kept them going.

Now, that's what I call indomitable spirit! The Wortman family certainly had what it takes to be castaways, didn't they? Each helped the others whenever possible, they gave 110 percent so they could all survive, and they kept one anothers' flagging spirits up. That's the sort of teamwork that is essential in a castaway situation.

Fact File

Frostbitten flesh turns black, shrivels up, and looks as if it will fall off. Yucky, I know, but, in some cases, life has been known to return to a frostbitten limb even after three to six weeks.

Castaway Know-how

If you're a castaway in an inhospitable climate, you will obviously need shelter, warmth, and food. You should also protect yourself against snow blindness. This condition is very painful and is caused by the glare from the sun on expanses of white snow.

• If you don't have protective goggles, you can improvise by using a handkerchief, scarf, or some other item of clothing, tied over your face, with tiny slits for each eye.

• Alternatively, you can use masking tape, mud, or even blood over your regular glasses so that just a small peephole is left through each lens.

• Use charcoal, soot, or mud to darken the area around your eyes, or if your hair is long enough, let it hang forward over your face for protection.

These measures work just as well against sun blindness. The symptoms of both conditions are the same — your eyes begin to feel scratchy. Then they start to burn, and things become fuzzy. The pain increases horrendously until finally you can no longer see. Luckily, if treated correctly, sun and snow blindness can be reversible.

DESERT ISLAND DISH

In the late 1990s, British television celebrity Joanna Lumley (of *Absolutely Fabulous* fame) agreed to be a castaway on a desert island for a week, and the adventure was televised to the nation. She had no experience of living in the rough, and this glamorous actress was prepared to be seen warts and all as she recorded the best and worst moments of her seclusion.

BARE ESSENTIALS

Joanna was allowed to take a few basic provisions with her, such as rice and matches to start a fire. The camera crew dropped her off on the deserted island and called in periodically to check that she was not in any danger. They would then leave again. They also left Joanna with a video camera to record the experience.

INGENUITY

Joanna discovered a dry, warm cave not far from the beach, and she decided to make her camp in the cave rather than build a shelter. Although the rock was rather hard to sleep on, at least she was warm. She made a fire in the mouth of the cave to boil water for her evening meal. With no artificial light to read by, she went to sleep when it grew dark and got up at dawn.

Bringing a touch of suburban comfort to her desert island, Joanna used a needle and thread to ingeniously convert her bra into a pair of slippers for padding around her cave — now that's what I call improvisation!

TOUCH OF LUXURY

Our castaway celebrity was allowed to take one luxury item with her on her trip, and Joanna chose watercolor paints and a pad of paper. She whiled away many a pleasant hour exploring her island home and recording it for posterity in watercolor sketches. It was a good choice, don't you think?

Joanna was pretty lucky in that the weather, on the whole, was very good, and there weren't any nasty beasts to contend with. She felt that the worst part of the experience was the monotony of the food — you can only eat so much boiled rice and vegetables and still enjoy it — and by the end, she was desperate for a decent meal. But she coped extremely well with the solitude and, overall, enjoyed her castaway experience.

WHAT IF . . .

If you were able to take one luxury item with you on your desert island, what would it be? Think hard before you choose. Don't forget that the batteries on a Game Boy or other electronic game would soon run out, and then it would be useless. Is there something else that gives you great pleasure and that you can enjoy time and time again? Why not give it some thought?

Fact File
The British public adored seeing this fly-on-the-wall documentary of a famous person up against adversity and having to cope on her own. So much so that Joanna's castaway program spawned a couple of follow-up documentaries. One celebrity was left in the jungle, and another was abandoned in grizzly-bear country!

CAVE DWELLERS
Caves can make very good shelters, as Joanna Lumley discovered, but because of this fact, you'll find all sorts of other critters sheltering in them. In particular, bats like to make their homes in the recesses of dark caves.

Most bats are completely harmless and eat only fruit, but the bats of the *Desmodontidae* family that live in South and Central America feed on blood!

These vampire bats, which grow to about three

and a half inches in length, feed on all kinds of mammals including horses, cattle, and occasionally humans. They fly low and settle on the ground before running to a victim. Then they slice a piece of skin from their sleeping prey, using their sharp incisor teeth, and lap up the flowing blood. The bite is painless, and the loss of blood is small, but if there were lots of bats feeding on one victim . . . who knows?

In their favor — because, let's face it, vampire bats get bad press — bats are one of the few mammals known to adopt orphans or to help other bats in need. So they're not all bad, after all.

CASTAWAY
COMMUNITIES

CASTAWAY COMMUNITIES

Somehow the thought of being a castaway in a group seems less frightening than being a sole survivor, doesn't it? Of course, it is easier to live as a castaway if there are several people to pool resources and ideas and to share the labor. Having company also boosts morale. But as we'll see in the coming stories, being a castaway with others brings a set of problems all its own.

To live in cramped conditions under physical, mental, and emotional stress puts a lot of strain on relationships with others. As a member of a castaway community, each person has to have respect for the others and to realize that everyone has a role to play and something to contribute to the group.

CASTAWAY 2000

At the start of the new millennium, a television project was conceived to examine what aspects of life are really important in society and what aspects could be disposed of. To do this, Castaway 2000 took a group of people representing a cross section of society and put them on a remote, isolated island to remove them from the everyday aspects of modern life.

WHO GETS TO GO?

The castaways were chosen with the help of a team of expert advisers after they answered an ad in the newspaper. More than 4,000 people applied, and the project chose twenty-eight adults and eight children to go to Tarensay, a Hebridean island off the coast of northern Scotland.

LAID LOW

However, the project got off to an inauspicious start, with half the community being struck down by flu within a week of arriving on the island. Since the accommodation was only half finished and the weather very bad, it was thought wise to take the sick people off the island to be treated and to convalesce on a neighboring inhabited isle.

This meant that only eighteen were left to battle the elements on their own and in very cramped, uncomfortable conditions. There was driving snow and gale-force winds that took the roof off the accommodation. Tempers were frayed, and there were several heated arguments, but the castaways muddled through.

NEW ARRIVALS

At the end of the first month, the remaining castaways took up their places on the island. The community moved into the three accommodation units (nicknamed pods) that were now completed, and the eight children studied their lessons in the farmhouse until the schoolhouse was finished.

In the second month, the community's livestock was delivered — three cows, one pony, forty chickens, a flock of sheep, and a family of pigs. The castaways also planted potatoes, carrots, and onions in poly-tunnels to guard against the volatile Scottish weather, and oats and barley were planted in the field.

The initial idea was that the livestock were to be raised for food, and a butcher was selected as part of the community. Yet as time passed, many of the castaways felt that they couldn't eat the animals they'd looked after, and an increasing number converted to being vegetarians. This caused a division in the community.

The other cause of a major dispute was that one of the three dogs that came to the island was pregnant when she arrived and subsequently gave birth, in the second month, to a litter of puppies. Some of the castaways wanted to keep the puppies as pets, while others felt the community couldn't support any more dogs. It's a hard call, isn't it? What would you have decided? Could you send the puppies away for the good of the community?

FACING CHALLENGES

Most of the castaways adjusted well to their new environment and harsh way of life. In fact, many were more concerned about adjusting back into "real" life at the end of the yearlong project — some didn't even want to return.

Most of all, the challenges that the castaways faced continued to force them to examine issues about what a community is and the values of society and to look at their own personal integrity and behavior. From dealing with a lack of living accommodation in the early days to reconciling the community budget or coping with the animals — all of these situations brought a wider reflection on life in general.

Fact File
The design for the tunnel-shaped accommodation "pods" on Tarensay was inspired by the Viking tradition of living under the upturned hulls of their Viking ships.

Castaway Know-how

Conflict Resolution: Whether you're in a castaway community or society at large, you must be able to settle your differences with others.

In a small castaway community where all the members rely on one another, it is even more vital that disputes are settled quickly. And it's no good waiting for a problem to arise — an agreed way of resolving problems should be put in place from the outset.

It stands to reason that people will have different opinions and objectives, but how to deal with these differences is most crucial. People may lose their temper in the heat of the moment, but the situation must be resolved calmly.

Each person should have a right to air their views and

put forward their side of the argument. As a community you have to agree on how a decision is made or a dispute settled. Is it put to a vote? Does the majority carry the decision, or must it be unanimous? Do you have a council to settle disputes? Whatever you choose, everyone must agree to stick to it. Even if it feels unjust, there is no benefit to dwelling on it and letting a grudge or grievance ruin your relationship with another member of the community.

If you respect other people's rights to hold views and opinions different from your own, then airing your differences and "burying the hatchet" always seems to clear the air and make everyone feel better.

MUTINY ON THE BOUNTY

In 1787, William Bligh, a young British naval officer, was commissioned to undertake a voyage to the Caribbean on a small ship named HMS *Bounty*.

The voyage was difficult, and ill feelings were common (like many voyages of the time, no doubt). After a long stay in Tahiti gathering and stowing breadfruit plantings, the *Bounty* began its voyage to the Caribbean and then back to England.

MUTINY

On the morning of April 28, 1789, twelve crew members, led by ship's mate Fletcher Christian, staged the now-famous mutiny, capturing the ship and setting Captain Bligh and his supporters adrift in the ship's launch.

The ship then sailed back to Tahiti to the friends and loved ones the crew had left behind. Christian knew they could not stay there because mutiny, in those days, was an offense that was punishable by hanging. So the mutineers and their Tahitian companions spent months sailing the seas, looking for somewhere to settle.

SETTLEMENT

On January 15, 1790, they finally settled on the tiny island of Pitcairn — an ideal location for mutineers. It had coconuts, breadfruit, fresh water, and most important, it was isolated, and they were unlikely to be found.

With pigs, chickens, yams, and sweet potatoes from the ship's stores, there was plenty to eat. They stripped the *Bounty* of all they could and then ran it ashore and set it on fire so there would be no evidence for any passing vessel that might be looking for them.

Of the mutineers, four died within four years of arrival. The Tahitians were treated poorly, and this led to a revolt in which four mutineers were killed. The Tahitians themselves were also killed. This left, in 1794, only Edward Young, Jack Adams, Matthew Quintal, and William McCoy, with the women and children.

The next four years were relatively peaceful and harmonious, until McCoy discovered how to brew a potent alcohol from the roots of the ti plant. Drunken bouts of temper ensued.

By 1799, Young and Adams had killed Quintal in

self-defense, and McCoy had drowned himself. Then, in 1800, Young died of asthma, leaving John Adams as the sole male survivor of the party that had landed just ten years earlier.

CASTAWAY COMMUNITY

Adams, as leader of the community of ten Polynesian women and twenty-three children, showed himself to be a capable, kind, and honest man. He could barely read and write, but he was revered for his pious and virtuous ways. Adams saw to it that every young person observed family prayers and a Sunday "church" service, cultivated the land, cared for the livestock, and did not marry until able to support a family.

In 1808, an American captain, Mayhew Folger, arrived, but his visit was brief and his report aroused little interest in England at that time. (They were too busy fighting Napoleon!)

However, six years later, two British navy vessels rediscovered the little community. Fortunately for Adams, the commanders were favorably impressed by him and the example he'd set, and they agreed that it would be "an act of great cruelty and inhumanity" to arrest him.

MISSIONARIES

Reports of the community reached Britain and stimulated much interest, particularly in the English Missionary Society. Gifts of Bibles, prayer books, and spelling books were sent to the island, as well as crockery, razors, tools, and guns. In addition, nearly every passing ship made generous gifts and bartered surplus supplies for fresh food, so that the way of life on the island became more European.

However, as he grew old, Adams worried about the future of his community. Eventually, John Buffett, a shipwright from England, and John Evans, a Welshman, landed on the island in 1823. Both married island women and founded families. Buffett taught the children and took over the church services from Adams.

By now, the population had increased to sixty-

Making Yourself Understood

When the crew of the _Bounty_ arrived in Tahiti, they set to work shoulder to shoulder with the Tahitian people. These seamen were living among the people of the island and had to find ways to communicate with those around them.

Soon a hybrid language called pidgin or patois developed so that both cultures could make themselves understood — and this process has happened wherever there has been extended contact between unrelated cultures.

On Pitcairn, pidgin became the primary means of communication and has developed into the Pitkern language that is still spoken today on the island.

six and on March 5, 1829, John Adams died at the age of sixty-two. To this day, he is known as "Father" by every member of the Pitcairn community.

YOU CAN SAY THAT AGAIN

How do you think you'd have done, trying to talk to the islanders? Would you have resorted to grunting, pointing, and smiling, or would you have had a go at conversing?

Well, why don't we see just how hard or easy it might be to understand pidgin. Here is a small speech that you might be greeted with when you arrive on an inhabited island near Papua New Guinea. See if you can make sense of it. You'll find a translation on the next page to compare with your efforts.

Apinun poren! Nem bilong mi Aruwee.
Mi wanpela bigman bilong dispela ples.
Mi hamamas tru olsem yupela i kamap long asples bilong mi.

Igat plenti pikinini bilong mi istap olsem tupela meri na tupela man. Oli hamamas tru long wokabaut wantaim yupela long ailan bilong mipela. Iorait sapos yupela i stap long ples bilong mipela. Long nait mipela kamapim wanpela singsing long yupela igat planti gutpela kaikai na mipela danis nabaut nabaut. Olsem, oli lik wokim belas.

So how did you do? I couldn't make head or tail of it, so I guess I need to practice. Hopefully, you did a bit better. Here's the translation, anyway:

Hello, friend, my name is Aruwee. I am the (number one) chief of this place. I am happy truly because you have come up to this place of mine. I have got children of mine staying here, two girls and two boys. All will be happy to walk about with you around our island. It will be all right, suppose you stay in the place that belongs to me. In the evening, I will create a sing-sing for you with plenty of good food, and we will dance. We like to dress up.

Just in case you find yourself a castaway in an island community that speaks pidgin, here are a few other useful phrases you might like to learn:

What is your name? = Wanem nem bilong yu?

How old are you? = Hamas Krismas bilong yu? (How many Christmases?)

My name is John. = Nem bilong me I John.

Do you have any food? = Yu gat kaikai I stap?

Where is the nearest McDonald's? = McDonald's I stap we?

Toilet/latrine/rest room? = Haus pekpek?

SHIPWRECKED

Somewhere in the middle of the Pacific Ocean lies the most beautiful island you are ever likely to see. Surrounded by the clearest turquoise water and soft white sand, Motorakau is an uninhabited heaven nestling among the Cook Islands.

In September 1999, armed with only a few essential items, sixteen people, all under the age of twenty-five, were left to survive on this desert island for ten weeks. With limited food and shelter, the castaways had to rely on one another to get by.

LIFE ON MOTORAKAU

Food was a constant source of stress for the castaways. Failure to catch fish meant rice and more rice for dinner. Desperation led some to eat snails. Things took a more macabre turn when attention turned to Gloria and Gaynor, two pigs on the island. After a protracted hunt, the castaways finally managed to capture Gaynor. But did they have the guts to kill her? What do you think?

Leadership was taken extremely seriously on the island. Each week a leader was democratically elected. He or she had absolute authority over the community, which inevitably led to raging arguments. Before they knew it, they had descended into treachery!

CHAPTER EIGHT

FRIEND OR FOE?

Claustrophobia was one of the biggest challenges facing the fledgling community. Motorakau is less than a half mile long, and it takes only fifteen minutes to stroll around the perimeter. It's 2,500 miles from the nearest mainland, and there is no way of getting away from it all, even when the bickering and boredom get to be too much.

Tensions within the group proved too much for some of the community members. One woman left after five weeks, and several more "escaped" on the provision boat to the mainland days before the conclusion of the project. In fact, only a handful saw the adventure through to its end.

In the aftermath, there were accusations and counteraccusations about people's behavior on the island. Feelings were obviously running very high.

It became clear that intense friendships and bitter rivalries existed within their castaway environment, and after a while, the community could not function as a team.

Oh, and in case you're wondering, they did kill Gaynor, but Gloria survived and was set free.

CHAPTER EIGHT

Teamwork: A community can only thrive if every member contributes to the best of his or her ability and finds a role to play. That doesn't mean that we all have to take control, making decisions and showing leadership qualities. In fact, if we all did that, the community would soon falter.

A good team consists of people who can offer a cross section of qualities. You need an idea person, but you also need practical, thorough people who can carry through an idea. A leader and decision-maker is useful, but so is someone who can communicate well or who can make people feel good about themselves. Whatever your character and personal qualities, there is almost certainly a role for you to play in a castaway community.

The following factors are important in an effective team:
- People trust one another
- Feelings are expressed freely
- Processing issues is part of the community's life
- Commitment is high
- Objectives are shared by all
- Listening is important
- Conflicts are worked through
- Decisions are made by consensus
- People are open to one another's ideas and feelings

CASTAWAY BRAIN-TEASERS

CASTAWAY BRAIN-TEASERS

You'll have plenty of time as a castaway to try to get your head around these tricky brain teasers. But you don't have to wait to be marooned to test them. Try them out at home to see how "castaway-wise" you are.

These teasers have tried the patience of many an outdoor specialist and expert all over the world. They are often used in training to test initiative and knowledge — so don't worry too much if you find them a bit tough. Let's see how you do, shall we?

SEPARATED FROM YOUR FELLOW CASTAWAYS

A large group is marooned on a remote, mountainous, hostile island. A small reconnaissance party of five (including yourself) sets out in good weather to explore the mountains. You've been camping out, but on the second night, the snow starts to fall, and it snows all the next day. Your party is trapped in their tent.

Visibility is down to about twenty yards, and a force-six northeasterly wind is blowing. Temperatures are falling, and while the snow coverage is two feet deep all over, drifting makes conditions treacherous.

You are faced with a series of choices. The weather shows no signs of improving, and one of the people in your group is beginning to suffer from hypothermia. It seems that your only chance of survival is to send one or more of your party to get help from the camp.

You have to decide:
1 how many of you should go
2 what equipment should you take
3 what should you leave with the tent

The choices you make could mean the difference between survival and disaster for you and the members of your group, so think hard.

You can choose ten items to take with you. The rest have to stay with the casualty. Put them in order of importance. If you think the flashlight is the most important item to take with you, put that at the top of your list and work your way down.

Give yourself fifteen minutes to choose your top ten. And good luck!

The equipment list is:
· Compass
· Tourist map of the island
· 4 sleeping bags, summer-weight
· 3 packets of soup
· Small first-aid kit
· Pocketknife
· 2 packets of fruitcake
· Matches in a waterproof container

· Book entitled *Advanced Scout Guide to Hiking*
· 4-battery flashlight
· 120-foot rope
· 4 Snickers candy bars
· Whistle
· Watch
· Ice ax
· Primus stove and fuel cylinder
· Large polyethylene bag
· 2 flares
· 2 backpacks

CHAPTER NINE

SOLUTION

Here are the experts' answers. Equipment to take in order of priority:

> 1. Compass — To find the way.
> 2. Map — To find the way.
> 3. Flashlight — To see the map, etc.
> 4. Polyethylene bag — To use as windshield.
> 5. Whistle — To give the distress signal of three blasts. Sound carries a long distance.
> 6. Rope — To tie the party together, to act as a recovery aid if anyone falls into a gully, etc.
> 7. Ice ax — Useful as a point; also to feel the ground in front of your party as you descend.
> 8. Snickers candy bars — A quick source of energy.
> 9. First-aid kit — Minor use, but of no use to the people in the tent.
> 10. Backpacks — To carry equipment; no use to the people in the tent.

Three people should go for help, preferably your best three navigators, leaving one person to look after the casualty.

So how did you do? Shall we do the scores and see if you're a Castaway Survivor or not?

SCORING

Add up the points for your ten answers (and add twenty-five more to your total if you had three people going for help), and then check out the results.

Compass — 12 points
Map — 11 points
Flashlight — 10 points
Polyethylene bag — 9 points
Whistle — 8 points
Rope — 7 points
Ice ax — 6 points
Snickers candy bars — 5 points
First-aid kit — 4 points
Backpacks — 3 points
Sleeping bags — 2 points
Packets of soup — 2 points
Pocketknife — 2 points
Fruitcake — 2 points
Matches — 2 points
Book — 2 points
Watch — 2 points
Primus stove — 2 points
Flares — 2 points

SCORES

76-100: The applause should still be ringing in your ears. Not only did you save yourself, but you saved all the others from your party, too. You'll make a strong Castaway Survivor.

51-75: Not bad at all. You probably made it back to base camp, and rather late for comfort, the other two up the mountain were rescued. A good first attempt.

26-50: Well, you and your two friends limp back

into camp, cold, wet, and smelly, but it may be too late for your poor pals up the mountain.

0-25: What can I say? It's back to the drawing board, I'm afraid, because none of you made it this time.

Fact File

You will always see maps and navigation tools high on the list of survival priorities, but if nobody in the party knows how to read a map or use navigation aids, their actual value to you is zero. You'd be better served using a map you can't read to light a fire!

TROPICAL CASTAWAY

You are one of a group of survivors from an airplane that has crash-landed on an inhospitable tropical island. You've each managed to salvage a personal possession, but you have to get to the other side of the island where there's fresh water and a deserted shelter that you can make into your castaway camp. You cannot cross the interior, so you make a leaky raft to paddle around the shore.

You all set off with your belongings. The raft is overcrowded and overloaded with people and their personal effects. You realize that very soon there will have to be a discussion to decide how the load can be lightened to increase everyone's chances of reaching the castaway camp.

Here's the list of items, their weight, and their

value. You have to rank, in order, the items that you think can be thrown overboard to reduce the load.

Person	Item	Weight	Value
Flight attendant	First-aid kit	6 lbs.	$30
Flight attendant	Case of canned fruit juice	14 lbs.	$18
Hollywood film director	Exposed movie film	30 lbs.	$1,500,000
Diplomat	Top-secret documents	6 lbs.	$?
Film cameraman	Movie camera	16 lbs.	$7,500
Film technician	Unexposed movie film	14 lbs.	$300
Film actress	Pet dog	10 lbs.	$150
Film actor	Portable tape recorder	14 lbs.	$120
Navigator	Air navigation charts	6 lbs.	$75
Pilot	Flashlight	1 lb.	—
Woman	Radio	5 lbs.	$45
Child	Suitcase of drying clothes	14 lbs	$75
Clergyman	Unique ancient religious manuscripts	8 lbs.	$?
Businessman	2 bottles whiskey	4 lbs.	$80
Archaeologist	Rare gold coins in briefcase	2 lbs.	$40,000
Dealer	Uncut diamonds	1 lb.	$300,000

Note: The pilot is seriously injured.

You have to rank the items in the order in which you think they should be thrown away. For example, if you think that the portable tape recorder is the most useless item and should be the first item to go, enter it in the space next to 1 on the list.

Rank	Item
1	
2	
3	
4	
5	
6	
7	
8	
9	
10	
11	
12	
13	
14	
15	
16	

This brainteaser is a great way to exercise your creative thinking. You might want to think about some alternative uses for some of the items before you decide to get rid of them. (Yes, that is a clue.)

CHAPTER NINE

If you put your heads together with a few friends over this puzzler, you'll see that, through the pooling of ideas, a group is often more likely to reach a reasoned decision than an individual. This is a good example of how a team can work well together to solve problems in a castaway situation.

Give yourself fifteen minutes to complete this exercise if you're working alone, or thirty minutes if you're discussing it with your friends.

SOLUTION

Did you find it tough? It's a harder decision when several factors have to be taken into account, isn't it? But when it's a life-or-death situation, you soon realize that financial value is of little consideration.

Let's see how you scored, shall we? Add up the score for your top eight choices:

1 Exposed movie film (30 lbs.)
Very heavy and not worth anything to you as castaways. However, if the cases are shiny, keep for signaling and paddling. Score: 1

2 Movie camera (16 lbs.)
Heavy and useless. Score: 1

3 Unexposed movie film (14 lbs.)
Same reasons as for (1) above. Score: 1

4 Tape recorder (14 lbs.)
Pretty heavy and no real use. But check to see if the batteries fit the flashlight before you throw them away. Score: 1

5 Religious manuscripts (8 lbs.)
No value to castaways except maybe as kindling to light a fire when you get to camp. Score: 2

6 Top-secret documents (6 lbs.)
No threat to security on an island — only possible use is tinder for fire. Score: 2

7 Radio (5 lbs.)
There are no transmitting frequencies, but it could keep you entertained briefly. Score: 2

8 Air navigation charts (6 lbs.)
Useless without navigational aids. It doesn't much matter where you are, but where your rescuers are. You might as well burn them. Score: 2

9 Suitcase of clothes (14 lbs.)
Use clothes for protection against sunburn and use suitcase for bailing and catching rainwater. Score: 5

10 Rare gold coins in briefcase (2 lbs.)
Not interested in the coins, but the briefcase could be useful for bailing, paddling, and catching rainwater. Score: 5

11 Whiskey (4 lbs.)
Alcohol dehydrates, so it would be disastrous to drink it, but it could possibly be used as an antiseptic for injuries. Score: 5

12 Rough diamonds (1 lb.)
Fairly light and could be used for cutting tools (diamonds are very hard). Score: 10

13 First-aid kit (6 lbs.)
You may well need this. Score: 10

14 Flashlight (1 lb.)
Light and useful. Score: 10
15 Dog (10 lbs.)
A bit heavy, but you'd have to be pretty hard-hearted to dump the dog unless you had to. If it comes down to a decision between a person and the dog, though, the dog goes. Score: 10
16 Canned fruit juice (14 lbs.)
Essential to replace lost fluid during hot days and to give you energy. Score: 10

TOTAL SCORE

51–65: Excellent. You stand a good chance of reaching the camp intact and with as many useful possessions as possible.
31–50: Good. You'll probably get there, but you'll be wet and tired, and you might have a few strange items with you when you arrive.
16–30: Fair. You're all going to be extremely thirsty, sunburned, and near exhaustion when you get to camp, but you should eventually make it — just!
15 or under: Lousy. Oops. A few bad decisions, it seems, so be prepared for a long swim!

SHIPWRECK

In forty minutes, your ship is going to sink. All the members of your group are safely inside a lifeboat, which can escape the disaster. There is enough food and fuel for several months. You can definitely reach a habitable but deserted island and start a castaway community, but the lifeboat and the island itself will be cramped, and there is little opportunity for privacy.

Your places in the boat are safe, and you cannot be asked to give them up. There are ten people outside the boat who are hoping to escape, and from these you must choose only five to fill the remaining places in the lifeboat. You are the only survivors. Choose from the following people:

1 Priest
Age thirty-five, a veteran. A quiet person who is often able to calm and comfort others.

2 Pregnant woman
Age twenty-five, and seven months pregnant. A good cook, she is in good health and expects a normal delivery.

3 Pregnant woman's husband
Age twenty-six. Runs a successful building business and is competent in all the basic construction skills.

4 Armed policeman
Age thirty-eight. Awaiting promotion to inspector. Trained in the use of firearms and electronic communications and commended for bravery after rescuing two people from a burning car. Leaving behind a wife and two children. Carrying a loaded pistol.

5 Football player
Age twenty-two, male. Well thought of as a football player. Has a knack for rallying the team when they seem demoralized or about to face defeat. Also trained as a butcher.

6 Nurse

Age twenty-five, male. Qualified in both general medical and psychiatric nursing. Leaving behind his partner with whom he's lived for five years.

7 Actress

Age twenty-two. Trained as a primary school-teacher before becoming a successful actress in TV comedies. Had a nervous breakdown four years ago.

8 Geologist

Age thirty-two, female. Has two children by a previous marriage, now divorced and working for a mining company identifying rock specimens.

9 Science student

Age twenty. Completed two years of a degree course in microelectronics and the use of computers.

10 Teenager

Age thirteen, female. Still at school and interested in sciences. Tends to be moody.

All ten people are physically and mentally fit unless stated otherwise.

It's a tough choice, isn't it? Why don't you and your friends sit down and work out who you should take and why. Give yourself twenty minutes or so, and then check the answers. (No cheating now — or you'll be out of the boat!)

SOLUTION

Well, this is a bit of a trick question, really. There are no wrong or right answers. You probably selected your five answers from the skills they could offer the castaway community, which is fair enough. However, as we saw in the last chapter, the personal qualities that someone brings to a team can be just as important as the specialist knowledge.

A doctor's medical knowledge is of little value if he spends his whole time saying, "We're doomed, doomed, I tell you" and he has no will to survive. Similarly, someone with no specialist skills might be brilliant at rallying the community's flagging spirits and exhibiting leadership qualities.

Who knows how any of us will react in extreme and unusual circumstances such as a castaway situation? But one thing is for sure — the right attitude of mind is what really counts.

Finally, here are two brainteasers that will give you some practice in analytical thinking and problem-solving — both useful skills when you're a castaway.

ANALYTICAL AGNES

Agnes, who is extremely analytical, has five friends. They each wrote a logic examination paper, and they were all pretty bright.

The names of her friends are Beatrice, Clarissa, Dolly, Erica, and Fanny. I am able to give you the following details of their places in the test (there were no ties):

- Dolly was one place higher than Agnes was.
- Beatrice was not first or last.

- Erica was two places higher than Clarissa was.
- Fanny's place was even, and Agnes's place was odd.

What were their places in the test? Give yourself a generous fifteen minutes to come up with the answer to this puzzler.

> **Solution**
> 1 Erica 2 Beatrice 3 Clarissa
> 4 Dolly 5 Agnes 6 Fanny

Did you get them in the right order? It's amazing how you can figure these things out if you just sit down and think logically for a while.

Want to try pitting your wits against another brainteaser? Well, try this one, but I warn you, it's a toughie.

WHO OWNS THE PARROT?

This tricky brainteaser can be solved using your powers of deduction, analysis, and sheer persistence — all essential qualities in the successful castaway.

There are five houses, each with a front door of a different color and inhabited by pirates of different nationalities, with different pets and drinks. Each pirate eats a different kind of fruit. Yo, ho, ho, me hearties — you're ready to start deducing.

- The English pirate lives in the house with the red door.
- The Spanish pirate owns the dog.
- Coffee is drunk in the house with the green door.
- The Ukrainian pirate drinks tea.
- The house with the green door is immediately to the right (your right) of the house with the ivory door.
- The Moroccan date-eater owns snails.
- Bananas are eaten in the house with the yellow door.
- Milk is drunk in the middle house.
- The Norwegian pirate lives in the first house on the left.
- The pirate who eats berries lives in the house next to the man with the fox.
- Bananas are eaten in the house next to the house where the horse is kept.
- The apple-eater drinks orange juice.
- The Japanese pirate eats melons.
- The Norwegian pirate lives next to the house with the blue door.

Now, who drinks water, and who owns the parrot?

SOLUTION

Well, shiver me timbers, did you work out that the Norwegian pirate drinks water and the Japanese pirate owns the parrot? Three cheers to those who got it right. The rest of you scabby sea dogs can walk the plank — sorry, I got carried away. . . .

Here are the rest of the answers to put your mind at rest if it proved too tricky for you.

Front doors	Yellow	Blue	Red	Ivory	Green
Inhabitants	Norwegian	Ukrainian	English	Spanish	Japanese
Pets	Fox	Horse	Snails	Dog	Parrot
Drinks	Water	Tea	Milk	Orange juice	Coffee
Fruit	Bananas	Berries	Moroccan dates	Apples	Melons

I always find that drawing up a table like this helps me to solve the riddle. It may well work for you, too.

YOUR
CASTAWAY
RATING

YOUR CASTAWAY RATING

I scarcely believe we've come all this way together since that first test. But just before we part company, there's one last thing I promised.

I said we'd have a final quiz to see whether you've been paying attention. Had you forgotten? So let's see how much you can remember, shall we? Oh, and if you're finding some of the questions a bit tough, you'll find that the answers are given throughout the book, so you can flick back through to refresh your memory if you like.

Now, pencils at the ready, let's go — and best of luck!

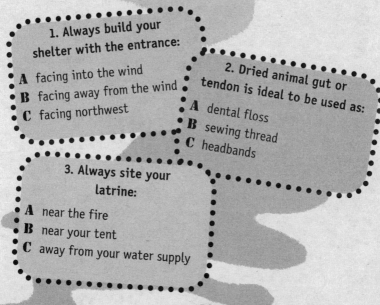

1. Always build your shelter with the entrance:

A facing into the wind
B facing away from the wind
C facing northwest

2. Dried animal gut or tendon is ideal to be used as:

A dental floss
B sewing thread
C headbands

3. Always site your latrine:

A near the fire
B near your tent
C away from your water supply

4. When it's wet, you can find dry deadwood:

A in the cracks and branches of trees or underneath bushes and piles of leaves
B in the long grass
C in running water

5. Bracken is safe to eat if it is:

A mature
B young
C loosely coiled

6. The edibility test is a way to check that:

A food is safe to eat
B food is the right temperature
C the password is Eddie

7. Insects and grubs taste best when cooked first. They are ready:

A when they wriggle
B when they are dry
C when they are black and smoking

8. You can eat the flesh of all mammals, birds, or reptiles with the exception of:

A toads
B frogs
C newts

9. Almost any signal is understood internationally as a distress signal if it is repeated:

A three times
B six times
C seven times

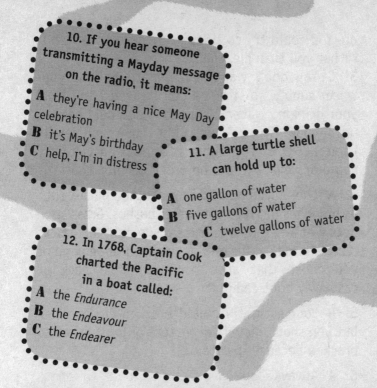

10. If you hear someone transmitting a Mayday message on the radio, it means:

A they're having a nice May Day celebration

B it's May's birthday

C help, I'm in distress

11. A large turtle shell can hold up to:

A one gallon of water

B five gallons of water

C twelve gallons of water

12. In 1768, Captain Cook charted the Pacific in a boat called:

A the *Endurance*

B the *Endeavour*

C the *Endearer*

ANSWERS

1. A Facing away from the wind.
Otherwise you'll have a cold and drafty shelter. If you believe in feng shui, then northwest is a good bet because this direction rules helpful people and travel — possible rescue? — but I think survival should be your first consideration, don't you?

2. B Sewing thread.
This sounds gross, but it is extremely useful for making and repairing shelters and clothes, and so

on. You could try to floss your teeth with it, but rather you than me, chum.

3. C You don't want anything to pollute your water supply, so site the latrine well away from your drinking water. I suppose you could have it near your fire or tent, but have you really thought this through? It's not particularly hygienic, and it would be pretty smelly, too!

4. A Look for dry wood in protected places such as branches of trees and under bushes. Grass soon gets wet and the water runs down onto any sticks lying around. As for running water, I hope none of you chose that answer or you'll be back at castaway boot camp.

5. B Young, tightly coiled bracken is delicious, but you should never eat mature or loosely coiled bracken because it is toxic.

6. A Always use the edibility test to check whether your food is safe to eat. The only test to see if food is the right temperature is to try it, but watch that you don't burn your tongue. Who needs a password when there's only you or a handful of you on the island?

7. B Grubs are cooked to perfection when they are dry. They might be a little underdone if you try them when they're still wriggling. And unless you like your food exceptionally well done, I'd eat them before they burn.

CHAPTER TEN

8. A Toads are poisonous. If there's anything wrong with eating frogs, someone had better tell the French — they've been eating frog legs as a delicacy for years. Newts are edible, but there isn't much meat on one.

9. A Any message repeated three times, whether it's a flash, a signal, or three fires, is understood as a distress signal. Any more than that and you'd run out of time, energy, and firewood.

10.C A Mayday message is a cry for help. Even if it's transmitted on May 1 or Auntie May's birthday, you should still take it to mean "I'm in distress."

11.C Believe it or not, large turtle shells can hold up to twelve gallons, which can be a lifesaver to a castaway.

12.B The *Endeavor*.

So, how did you do? I'm confident that you got most of the answers right. That means that in the unlikely event of you becoming a castaway — air and sea travel is extremely safe these days, so please don't have nightmares — you'll be in a good position to make the most of your situation.

Nonetheless, some people are now actively turning their backs on modern civilization and are deciding to go back to a simpler and more natural way of life in a self-imposed castaway situation.

CHAPTER TEN

The Lucy Irvines of this world and the Castaway 2000 volunteers are not alone in wanting to opt out of the rat race and to taste adventure.

If this option appeals to you and your family, I am comforted to know that you'll be better prepared to face the rigors of a castaway lifestyle after our adventure together.